Who Rules the School Now?

Paul Cookson is married to Sally and they live in Retford with their two children, Sam and Daisy. When he isn't visiting schools to perform his poems, Paul edits anthologies like this (his eighteenth for Macmillan). When not editing anthologies like this one, he writes poems for other anthologies like this. When not writing poems for other anthologies like this, he tries to write poems and stories for his own books. Usually he ends up playing five-a-side football, reading or listening to music instead.

Adventurous **Steven Hanson** was born, raised and still lives in Huddersfield. He is married to Lisa, and they have two daughters, Taome and Eden. A versatile illustrator and writer, Stephen's career includes film, animation, advertising, computer games and his own book, *Froobie Pink and the Night Noises*. He has never been a teacher and never intends to be one.

Other books from Macmillan

Who Rules the School?

Poems chosen by Paul Cookson

You're Not Going Out Like That!

Poems chosen by Paul Cookson

What Shape is a Poem?

Poems chosen by Paul Cookson

The Very Best of Paul Cookson

Poems by Paul Cookson

Spill the Beans

Poems by Paul Cookson and David Harmer

WHO RULES THE SCHOOL NOW?

Poems chosen by Paul Cookson

Illustrated by Steven Hanson

MACMILLAN CHILDREN'S BOOKS

To David, Claire, Oliver and Harriet

First published 2003 by Macmillan Children's Books
a division of Macmillan Publishers Limited
20 New Wharf Road, London N1 9RR
Basingstoke and Oxford
www.panmacmillan.com

Associated companies throughout the world

ISBN 0 330 39975 6

1 3 5 7 9 8 6 4 2

A CIP catalogue record for this book is available from the British Library.

Printed and bound in Great Britain by Mackays of Chatham plc, Kent

'Girl Power' by Les Baynton first published in *Are You sitting Comfortably?*, ed.
Brian Moses, Macmillan Children's Books, 2002. 'Playing with Fire' by Coral
Rumble first published in *Creatures, Teachers and Family Features* by Coral
Rumble, MacDonald Young Books, 1999.

Contents

The Arrogant Fire Alarm

They shut me in a glass prison – the fools.
But even here
I rule this school
And all must obey me
Without question.

Want proof?
See that boy struggling with his maths problem;
That teacher reciting a poem
The head reaching for his tea.

Listen.
I flex my electric muscle
And press my head against the window of my cell
My spine trembles
I feel a buzz and a click
And I break into my one-note song
NAAAAAAAAAAAAAAAAAAAAAAAAH!

Watch
Maths, poetry and tea
Abandoned
A whole school
Walking sensibly to the playground
Marching to the tune
Of my one-note song
NAAAAAAAAAAAAAAAAAAAH!

Now
I allow them to return
The problem is forgotten
The poem has lost its power
The tea is cold
All because of my one-note song
NAAAAAAAAAAAAAAAAAAAH!

John Coldwell

Signs Rule Our School

Headteacher's Office tells the head where to go
and Matron tells matron – you'd think they would know!

The Cloakroom sign tells us where to hang our cloaks
and Notice Board tells where to pin silly jokes.

Staffroom shows staff where to go for their tea
and Toilet signs tell where to go for a *

Kitchen tells cooks where to boil up our gruel
and Theatre shows where we may act the fool.

Classroom shows pupils where to mess about
and when the day's done Exit points the way out.

* Anyone got a rhyming dictionary?

Philip Waddell

Rumours Rule the School

Our headmaster Mr Pugh
Kissed our teacher, sweet Miss Drew
Hannah had a perfect view
From outside the Y6 loo
Clare and Rachel saw it too
They told me, now I've told you
Pass it on, it's really true.

Our bossy cook, Mrs Smew
Put frogs and spiders in the stew
Mixes treacle tart with glue
And lizard droppings from the zoo
Makes us eat the awful brew
Jack and Billy heard that too
Pass it on, it's really true.

Did you know that Mr Bigg
Our caretaker, wears a wig?
On windy days he hangs on tight
To stop it flying out of sight.
Time loves Jade and she loves Paul
Paul loves Clare who hates them all.
It was Dean who wrote those names

On the school wall during Games.
What a naughty so-and-so.
All of this is true you know.

The corridor outside Class Two
Is haunted by a grey ghost who
Makes you jump by shouting BOO!
It howls and wails, walks straight through
The doors and walls right next to you
Clocks turn back, light bulbs unscrew
Pass it on, it's really true.

Kyle put paint in Kieron's shoe
When he was in the dinner queue
Kieron didn't have a clue
Why his socks had turned bright blue
But thanks to me he soon knew
You see I told him it was you
Pass it on, it's really true.

Pass it on, pass it on, pass it on
It's really true.

David Harmer

The Day that Miss Went Missing and Sir Just Wasn't There

Classroom six completely changed
The furniture was rearranged
The atmosphere was different, something new was in the air
Playtime started way too soon
And lasted till the afternoon
The day that Miss went missing and Sir just wasn't there.

Where the blackboard should have been
There's a giant TV screen
Dayglo cartoons hypnotize with fluorescent glare
Lessons all were history
No English, Maths or Geography
The day when Miss went missing and Sir just wasn't there.

All computers have been set
For surfing on the Internet
Fingers click on keyboard and printers start to whirr
There's burger bars and takeaways
Where there once were art displays
The day that Miss went missing and Sir just wasn't there.

Lined along one classroom wall
Pool and snooker and pinball,
Along with table football for everyone to share
There's a video arcade
Flashing, crashing as it's played
The day that Miss went missing and Sir just wasn't there.
A thudding, scudding baseline pounds
Speakers quake and shake the grounds
Strobe lights strike like lightning as the rhythm starts to blare
Posters and graffiti art
Replace the Maths and spelling chart
The day that Miss went missing and Sir just wasn't there.

Look your best and feel real cool
With sun beds and jacuzzi pool
Complete with beauty salon for manicures and hair
Hoops for playing basketball
Hang tall on every classroom wall
The day that Miss went missing and Sir just wasn't there.

Instead of desks there's fruit machines
Instead of text books – magazines
Instead of hard-backed benches they all have a comfy chair
The only homework seems to be
Soaps and game show on TV
The day that Miss went missing and Sir just wasn't there.

The old regime was obsolete
When our arrangements were complete
The old was out, the new was in, so teachers just beware!
Pupil power rules this school
To make it fun and make it cool
The day that Miss went missing and Sir just wasn't there.

Paul Cookson

Girl Power

He was King of the Playground,
Lord of the Lunchbreak . . .
Always in the winning team,
Always first out, last back in
His voice was teacher-loud
His shouts bounced and echoed
Off the playground walls
His kicks fired the ball like a missile
Across the seething playground
And his tackles turned you over
With the force of a giant wave
All the small fry, the little fish
Looked up at him with admiration
And a little fear

Then something happened,
One scorching summer lunchtime
With footballers all bare chested
Like Brazilians on the beach
And girls flitting and floating
In butterfly-bright summer dresses
The King had hammered in a super goal
Hard, unstoppable . . . a winner all the way,
His small fans laughed and cheered
Ran to pat the wonderful back,

But one girl didn't, just his age
And just as tall, she tossed her ginger hair
Walked across the yard
And stood scowling right in front of him

YOU'VE HAD YOUR TIME . . .
YOUR FOOTBALL MATCH
ME AND THE GIRLS WANT TO DANCE
SO SHIFT OK
He breathed in hard, muttered something bad
And moved closer to the upstart girl
Then unflinching, she spoke in a voice
Just as loud as his . . .

I'VE TOLD YOU ONCE NOW SHIFT
ANY CLOSER AND YOU'LL GET
A GREAT BIG JUICY KISS

He turned away with angry eyes
And glowing cheeks, and a group of girls
Exploded the quietness into cheers and jeers

On other lunchtimes
He still struts arrogantly around,
But we all know that something has changed
And the King seems a little smaller

Les Baynton

The Man with the Mighty Finger

Down in the dark, dark depths
of the Education Office sits
the man with the all-powerful finger.
He presses a button
and in two hundred schools
on an exact day, at a precise time,
summer begins
– and the heating goes off.

We have
hailstorms, freak snow showers,
mornings still chilled by frost
but
it doesn't matter.
It is summer.
The man with the all-powerful finger
says so.

Then, on some October day,
which may be full of sun
or cold and dull,
the mighty digit hovers
presses,

radiators burp
and winter begins.
On-off, off-on.
Oh, the strange, alien power
of the man with the mighty finger
as we shiver and swelter
behind panes of glass
thinking
how much better it might be
if he could control
the weather.

Patricia Leighton

Down the Plughole

In the corner of our classroom,
down the plughole, in the sink,
lives a very noisy monster
who likes powder paint to drink.

He also loves those jelly blobs
of glue in yogurt pots –
the ones with paint brush bristles
in and papier mâché clots.

The more that he appreciates
his food the more he slurps –
he also glugs and gurgles and
does REALLY ripping burps.

But when this morning Tracey Watts
fed him her apple core,
he banged the pipes so hard they rocked
with clammerings for more.

The more he had, the more he clanked,
till we made him a potion,
of teacher's tea and lemonade,
which caused a small explosion.

The plughole plopped and then it glopped,
and something nasty spurted –
so the classroom was abandoned
and the caretaker alerted.

They let us back this afternoon –
the caretaker had been,
for his cap was on the drainer
and the sink was sparkling clean.

But the pipes were purring softly –
so I looked into the sink,
and thought I saw a little eye
look back at me – and wink . . .

Liz Brownlee

Fear My Name – Wet Break

The teachers work hard all morning
And the kids haven't made one mistake
When the words boom over the tannoy
My name is
WET BREAK

And you stare through the misty windows
As the playground becomes a lake
That's me – the spoiler of all fun
And my name is
WET BREAK

Yes I'm the living nightmare
From which none of you awake.
Fifteen minutes more in class
And my name is
WET BREAK

I am the one who pupils fear
I make the teachers quake
Because I steal their freedom
And my name is
WET BREAK.

John Coldwell

Who's the Richest Now?

The staff are in the classrooms
With the children working hard,

The caretaker whistles happily
Picking litter in the yard,

The headteacher's in his office
And he's feeling rather stunned,

The secretary's in Jamaica
Now she's stolen the school fund.

Ian Bland

Parents' Evening

Better get away and get away quick
Mum and Dad are soppy and I feel sick
But I can't get away, I feel so harassed
Mum and Dad are snogging and I'm so embarrassed.

It started with Dad tickling Mum
And then she couldn't stop wriggling
Then he whispered something rude
And soon they both were giggling.

Before too long she held his hand
And then he stroked her knee
A moment later things had gone
From bad to worse for me . . .

The silence then was shattered
With a loud resounding SMACK!
Dad puckered – Mum suckered
And began the snog attack.

Like two wrestling sink plungers
Glugging like a blocked-up plug
Or two greedy snuffling pigs
Slopping at a greasy slug.

I tried to hide from their wide
Embarrassing romantics
But they carried on regardless
With their amorous frantic antics . . .

Like two vacuum cleaners
On maximum full suction
Or two passionate octopi
Without an interruption.

They didn't seem to breathe at all
But gasped and gulped mid kiss
Their lips forever sealed
Like two glued jellyfish.

All that squashing, all that squelching,
All that slurpy sloshing
All the dripping, all the drooling,
Everyone was watching.

It wouldn't have been so bad
If the room was dark and dull
But it was my school Parents' Evening
The hall was lit . . . and jam-packed full!

If no one knew my parents
Then I wouldn't have to worry
But Dad is the headmaster
And Mum's the secretary!

Paul Cookson

Virus Rules K.O.

Please, please, please
be near them, when they sneeze.
Breathe in, breathe in . . .
Yes! Now my work begins:
so many times you'll blow your nose,
until it's redder than a rose.
I've found a perfect place to play,
inside your chest – my holiday!
Infest, infect and spread disease
and soon there's 'flu
for all of you:
The Register is full of crosses –
now you know who the real school boss is!
A hacking cough,
a week-long wheeze,
is just the stuff, so
please, please, please
be near them, when they sneeze, sneeze,
sneeze.

Mike Johnson

Beware of the School Nurse

Dan Smith had to visit our school nurse
He went in well and he came out worse
She sat him on a couch and jabbed him with a pin
To see what state his nerves were in
She stuck her hand in his mouth
And counted his teeth
Then lifted his tongue to inspect underneath
She rolled up his trousers and tapped him on the knee
And asked him if he went to the toilet regularly
She took out a torch and shone it in his eyes
And placed a ruler by each ear to measure their size
She sighed and said, 'Son you're in a terrible way.
You shouldn't have come to school today.'
'Stop,' said Dan. 'The Head sent me
To ask you to make him a cup of tea.'

John Coldwell

Who Rules the School?

The answer's really easy
School rulers rule the school,
They measure what we're doing
They like to rule us all!

Pencils are important
Governors as well
Parents and computers
Teachers, books and bells

Cleaners are essential
Dinner ladies shout

But headteachers
Do not rule much
   'cos they are always
        OUT.

Peter Dixon

My Name is Term

My name is Term.
I fix the dates.
I decide when the school is open
And when it is to be closed.

Three times a year
I bring an end to holidays
And summon teachers and pupils
Back to their desks.

Within my boundaries
The school is a hive of activity.

When I am over
The corridors are empty
And the classrooms silent.

I am Term.
I bring the school to life.

John Foster

Bert

The headmaster called him Mr Poole
but to everyone else he was Bert.
The word *Caretaker*'s right – he really cared,
nothing was too much trouble for him.

Bert,
My ball's on the roof, this downspout's bust,
a kid's been sick, could you bring sawdust?

He always wore the same flat cap
and when he opened up the school for the kids
he usually made the same joke about
opening the prison for business again.

Bert,
This doorknob came off in my hand.
Could you help me fix this jumping stand?

And when he retired after twenty-eight years
we bought him a smashing telly and
we all cheered him in the hall. It was
the only time I saw him without his cap.
Then there was this daft picture in the
local rag showing Bert handing over

his bucket and broom to the headmaster.
Then a fortnight later we heard he was dead.

Bert,
Could you come? A key's stuck in our lock
And could you please wind our classroom clock?
There's this to fix and that to mend . . .

No use to call, no use to send.

Eric Finney

SATs

Sir Announces Test.
Says, 'Children, do your best.'

'Good, no one is away.'
Some Agony Today.

'One hour and a quarter.'
Suffering And Torture.

'Minutes left . . . two.'
Soon All Through.

'I'm sure you did your best.'
Stinky Awful Test.

Eric Finney

We Are the Tests

We are the tests that you must pass.
We decide who's top of the class.

We are the tests which tell how well
You're able to read and write and spell.

We are the tests. We find out too
Which maths questions you can do.

We are the tests. We're able to show
Which scientific facts you know.

We are the tests. You needn't be scared
So long as you are well prepared.

We are the tests examining you.
We will discover if it's true

That you have worked, not played the fool.
We are the tests. We rule the school.

John Foster

The Totally Stonkering, Completely All-Conkering, Champion of the School

Don't care if it rains, if it's misty and damp
At full-on conkering I'm the champ
Rattle those branches, shake them free
Those little green hedgehogs high in the tree.

Open them up, all brown and shiny
Keep all the big ones, throw away the tiny
Grab a big bagful, get home quick
Getting good and ready, that's the trick!

I soak them in vinegar, bake them dry
Paint them with superglue, I really try
To toughen them, roughen them, set them hard
Then I'm the champion of the yard.

On Monday morning, I'm the first
With my Super-conkers I'm going to burst
Everybody else's weedy tries
Smash them, bash them down to size.

Rugged as a rock, really hard wearing
That's because of the big ball-bearing
Stuck in the middle of my best conker
It's a real winner, wow what a stonker!

My next best bet is this hundred and one-er
Get that cracking, a so-solid stunner
Knock down their conker, break it completely
I stamp it to powder, then smile sweetly.

I'm the school champion, there's no doubt
They jump up and down, they scream and shout
Don't like it when they lose but they always do
I'll take on anybody, how about you?

David Harmer

Who's Really in Charge?

Mr Thomas is the headteacher at our school.
No doubt.
His name is written very clearly on his office door.

You can tell he's the boss by the way he says:

WALK ON THE LEFT!
DON'T ANSWER ME BACK!
STAND OUTSIDE MY DOOR!
GO AWAY I'M BUSY!

But when Miss Patterson comes along to talk to him
he changes. It's all:

Oh yes Miss Patterson, good point!
And
Yes Miss Patterson I'll see to it right away!
And
Come in Miss Patterson, take a seat!

I wonder who the real boss is at our school?

Ian Bland

Watts Up

A simple fuse,
OK, that's me,
but treat me gently
or you'll see
a shocking end of energy.

It's me who rules
the school, you know,
because I am just
about to blow!

Mike Johnson

The Master Plan

The school stands dark and empty
the doors are locked up tight
they've moved on to the new school
where they'll learn to read and write.

But if you listen closely
if you listen hard
you just might hear some noises
as you stand there in the yard.

The rats have been learning Metalwork,
Chemistry, Maths and French.
The Caretaker's cat taught Biology
after being tied to a woodwork bench.

They mastered Physics in half a week
Engineering in less than a day
the rats have taken over the school
but that's not where they'll stay.

In the hall they've built a rocket
their master plan unfurled
taking the school was easy
now they want to rule the world.

Damian Harvey

Paper Chase

In a place called Bureaucratic,
legislation rules this school,
as teachers scribble, thinking –
'What for, and why?' – 'It's cruel!'

These forms must be completed,
amidst Staffroom groans and pleas,
statistics of officialdom
in perfect jargon-ese.

Piles of paper rule this school,
sent off in apprehension.
If they're not filled in properly –
the teacher gets Detention.

Stewart Henderson

Me! I Teach PE

Me! I teach PE
Not History or Geography, Maths or English or RE
PE! That's me!
Not Chemistry, Biology, Physics, Drama, CDT
PE! That's me!
Not French or German, PSE or Soci – poncy – ology
PE! That's me!

The subject of the gods – because it's taught by me
Bronzed and bold and beautiful – Me! I teach PE!

Whatever the weather is weather for sports
Football pitch or tennis courts
All year round I wear my shorts
I wrote one sentence on reports

A mine of sporting general knowledge
Go on ask me who
Scored the winner in the FA Cup of seventy-two.
Who scored the only single try at Twickers eighty-three?
I'll tell you what and where and why 'cos me I teach PE

Watch *Question of Sport* on BBC
PE! That's me!
The Midweek Match on ITV
PE! That's me!
Permanent action – B Sky B
PE! That's me!

I don't like fat kids, don't like weeds
Pigeon toes or knobbly knees,
Kids in glasses, kids who wheeze
Do not give me wimps like these!

Sport's the only crucial thing
Numero Uno – that is me
PE Rules and I am king
The man in charge – I teach PE

It's great to teach this subject
I know I teach it well
It's great to teach a subject
That even I can spell . . .

PE! That's me!

Paul Cookson

Snooze Rules

So what do teachers really do
When they get home from school?
Do they stay all strict and stern
Or do they act the fool?

Do they sit around in suits
Or do they sit in vests?
Do they talk of films and sports
Or is it books and desks?

But really, when you think of it,
The answer's not too deep –
After looking after thirty kids
They just fall fast asleep . . .

Clive Webster

Monster on the Wall

It rules the class from on the wall
Its size and weight scares us all.
It's huge, ugly, mean and black
And no one knows when it'll attack.

Inside its massive belly
Are things like tapioca, sprouts and jelly.
It stores lots of nasty things
Tarantulas, mosquitoes and bee stings.

It boasts of strange and yukky stuff
Like intestines, vomit and dandruff.
It threatens us with frightening thoughts
Of diseases, medicines, surgeons and warts

It'll jump down and shout we're wrong
It'll say we've got our words too long.
It'll tell us we've got letters mixed up
But we daren't ask it to shut up.

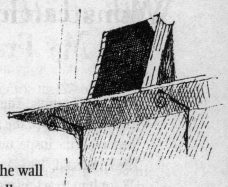

It rules the class from on the wall
Waiting for the teacher's call
On its shelf, always in sight
The dictionary that's always right.

Julie Hay

With a Little Help from My Friends

OFSTED's coming! The word got out
And terror gripped the school.
'Just a routine inspection',
The Head said, 'let's keep cool'.
OK for him to act relaxed,
He didn't teach 4C:
An awkward, stroppy lot they were
And they were down to me.
OK, maybe I feel for them
A weird kind of affection
But catch them in a Monday Mood
And I'd have a bad inspection.
Friday, before the Big Event,
My classroom after lunch:
Six of them, three boys, three girls
Huddled in a bunch.
Two at least from the Awkward Squad
Including Linda Best –
Voted in the Staffroom as
All-Time Number One Pest –
Talking their little heads off,
Really into some nitty-gritty.
'What's this then, Linda?' – she's in charge.

'Please Miss, it's a committee.'
Me, slightly sarky tone, 'Oh yes.
What's your committee's aim?'
Six sheepish grins but no reply.
'Come on, Linda, what's your game?'
'Please Miss, it's embarrassing.
I think we'd rather not say.'
Let them get away with that?
Teachers don't – no way!
'Let's risk the embarrassment, Linda.
What's the conspiracy?'
She looked all round the little group
To see if they'd agree.
Nods and mutters. 'OK Miss,
It's this Inspection thing.'
She'd got my full attention now –
Definitely interesting!
'We think it's getting you down a bit.
You're looking all gloomy glum.
So we're thinking up ways to make you look good
When the Inspectors come.'

Eric Finney

The Plumber's Plunger

Weeks of drips and ploppy drops
can drive you mad – until they stop.
No school survives without a plumber:
ring me now, you know my number.
Think, next time you take a drink,
who unblocks drains, cleans sinks that stink?
Only I can staunch that stench,
with my plumber's plunger and this wrench,
worth more than a priceless jewel.
Flush 'em gush 'em – rule the school!

No more showers, after PE,
no more Art (no teachers' tea);
in winter, you'd freeze to the spot –
I help keep radiators hot.
What do you do, if toilets leak?
That's right, I'm the one you seek:
only I can staunch that stench,
with my plumber's plunger and this wrench,
worth more than a priceless jewel.
Flush 'em gush 'em – rule the school!

Mike Johnson

VISITORS BEWARE!
IT'S THE SECRET
STAFFROOM CHAIR!

In the corner of the staffroom,
well worn and threadbare –
the booby-trapped, elastic-snapped,
collapsing secret chair.
Teachers leave it well alone,
they know what's lurking there . . .
the buttock-clenching, jacket-wrenching
never-mentioned chair.

The only seat that's left at break
so trying to relax
you sink in the ever-shrinking
chair apt to collapse.
Your coffee cup shoots ten feet up,
your knees are in your hair
in the folding, overloading,
self-imploding chair.

Every single time you move
it makes a little creak
the chair that makes staff stop and stare
at your every squeak.

It's like a black hole out in space
with cushions like a swamp
so wallow in the bottom-swallowing
chair that likes to chomp.

When sitting with the teachers
all visitors beware –
the jacket-wrenching, buttock-clenching,
ever-sinking, ever-shrinking,
self-imploding, overloading,
parping, squeaking, trouser-tweaking,
twisting, turning, non-discerning,
living, breathing, most deceiving,
booby-trapped, elastic-snapped,
collapsing staffroom chair.

Paul Cookson

School Chef

I'm Chef. Don't mess.
I've cooked with the best –
McDonald's and BK and more.
I'm Chef. Don't mess.
I'm tougher than the rest.
I cooked in the Vietnam War.

I'm Chef. Don't mess.
I've passed all the tests.
I know how to boil and fry.
I'm Chef. Don't mess.
I ain't got time for jests.
I can even make salad, if I try.

I'm Chef. I'm hard.
I use a lot of lard.
So don't expect to live for very long.
I'm Chef. I'm tough.
I've been here for long enough
Not to worry when a recipe goes wrong.

I'm Chef. I'm a twit.
I fry my chips in spit.
It gives them all the sogginess you hate.
I'm Chef. I'm evil.

I make my mince with weevils.
So pile it right up high upon your plate!

I'm Chef. I'm mad.
My cooking's really bad
And I think I might have poisoned quite a few.
I'm Chef. I'm insane.
I've got cooking on the brain.
And if I get ill, *so will you.*

Tom Wilde

No Escape

School smells
school smells
you can't get away
from school smells:

    strong whiffy polish
    as each term begins
    Miss Gee's killer perfume
    waspy waste bins
    odorous waftings
    outside the boys' loos
    manky PE kit
    lost property shoes

    sandwiches (mouldy)
    at the back of school trays
    sweat-reeking bodies
    on hot, sunny days
    nose-tingling, head-tingling
    new felt-tip pens
    pear drops, secretly shared
    with your friends.

Old Mr Whittaker's
peppermint breath
his zombie tweed jacket
as musty as death
curry and cabbage
vomit and bleach
cobwebs on cupboards
high out of reach.

No way to escape them
always they're there
those special school smells
in that special school air.

Patricia Leighton

The Photocopier

Out poured worksheets. Piles and piles
of photocopies. Miles and miles
of paper, covered with announcements,
notes to parents, Head's pronouncements.
The photocopier ran the school,
a useful and respected tool
used by pupils and by teachers,
possessing many useful features,
printing reams in black and white,
churning sheets out day and night.
Until the day it spouted rhymes,
multiplied a thousand times,
insulting odes about the staff
which made delighted pupils laugh,
a limerick about the Head
which made him curse and turn bright red
and heaps of haikus, rather rude,
about the school cook, Gertie Frood.
It besmirched the name of Governor Grimes
with twenty thousand vulgar rhymes,
then composed a shocking roundelay
which ridiculed the PTA.
The caretaker, grim Jasper Moon
was, in sonnet form, lampooned,

and dinner ladies, Flo and Jane
were gobsmacked by a sly cinquain.
Then overheated, overloaded,
the photocopier exploded
and the school came to a grinding halt.
All the photocopier's fault.

Marian Swinger

Playing with Fire

Never cross our caretaker,
Never make him mad,
Never call him names
Or tell him that he's sad;
Never steal his tools,
Never nick his screws,
Never spike his coffee
While he's listening to the news;
Never laugh at his overalls
Even though they're baggy,
Never tell him that his tummy's
Getting rather saggy;
Never stay in the cloakroom
When he's trying to sweep,
Never make loud noises
When he's just gone off to sleep;
Never stuff your litter
Underneath his cupboard door,
Never drop your chewing gum
Upon his polished floor;
Never write your name upon
A desk with pen or pencil,

Never decorate his bucket,
Even with a stencil;
Never complain loudly
When his radio starts to boom,
'Cause he'll feed you to the dragon
He keeps in the boiler room!

Coral Rumble

Di Caretaker's Ole Fatefull Klock

But stop!
There seems to be an item
Everybody forgot.

A mi! seh wen di Skool open,
An wen di Skool lock.

A mi! in charge widout a doubt,
As mi sen out mi daily scout.
If mi decide nu fi shout,
Di whole Skool a go lock out.

Mi nu even go a Skool;
A job like fimi, just got to be cool.
Mi laze around, an watch time pass by,
Mi nu even need a alibi.

Thru day and night, a mi! keep watch.
A mi! remind mi servant, fi open di lock.
A mi! rule di Skool, seh mi a di top notch.

A mi! di one an only, caretaker's klock.

Donavan Christopher

Fatefull = fathful	A Mi = I/me	Fi = to
Nu = not/don't	Fimi = mine	

Clocks Rule the School

'That clock can't be right,' thought Miss Pomfrey.
'It's got to be home time. It's slow.'
'That clock must be wrong,' muttered pupils.
'We're bored and we can't wait to go.'
The Head sighed and glared at the clock hands.
'Quarter past three. Is that all?'
and she strode from her office to check out
the time on the clock in the hall.
The caretaker glanced at his watch

It was twenty past three. Hip Hooray
Soon all those brats and those teachers
would be off for the rest of the day.
The clocks ran the school. They ticked softly
and precisely, and at half past three
the bell rang and clock-watching pupils
picked up their bags and were free.

Marian Swinger

The Mean Librarian

The mean librarian
gives us dirty looks,
makes us wash our hands
before we touch the books.
Hates us coming in,
says we make a noise.
Thinks we can't read,
says, 'Books are not toys.'

She stamps out our books
like she's stamping on our toes.
Always says, as if we wouldn't,
'Take good care of those.'

The mean librarian
checks in our returns.
Looks inside them carefully
for crumbs and stains and burns.
Slaps them on the counter
as if she's slapping faces,
then takes care to put them
in proper numbered spaces.
The mean librarian
will be satisfied when
all the books are safe on shelves
and never borrowed again!

Angela Topping

The Hayfever Rap

This is the hayfever rap –
I betcha know what I mean –
When your body needs a dose
Of antihistamine!
If the weather is dry
And there's a tickle in your nose
Very soon you'll find
The irritation grows.
When you're sniffin' and sneezin'
And you can't stop streamin'
Then your eyes start itchin'
    Till you feel like screamin'
    Do the hayever rap,
     The hayfever rap,
     The need-my-eyedrops-and-my-
      nasal-sprayfever rap!
     Be prepared for trouble
     In the warm days of June –
     Hey, even you teacher guys
     Are not imm-une!
     When there's pollen about
     Or you wanna cut the grass

Please think about the sufferin'
You'll cause in my class –
Don't start the hayfever rap,
The hayfever rap,
The half-the-kids-and-teachers-are-awayfever rap!
The (atishoo!) rap,
The (sniffle! sniffle!) rap,
The hay-hay-hay-hay-hay-hay-hay-hay-HAYfever rap!

Sue Cowling

The School Administrator

Who has all the Blu-tack hidden in her files
Who has pens and pencils in secret little piles
Whose face is like a lemon and never ever smiles . . .

Who has all the paper clips behind her lock and key
Who has all the chalk, the coffee and the tea
Who stocks all the Sellotape where nobody can see . . .

Who's the one who everyone is always berating
Who never offers cups of tea, keeps visitors all waiting
Who always has the final word 'cos she's intimidating . . .

Who dots every single *i* and crosses all the *tees*
Who only answers staff requests when they're on bended
   knees
Whose glare above her spectacles can make inspectors
   freeze . . .

Don't visit her when you are poorly
She's busy with her in-ven-tory
Don't ever try to get a plaster
You will never sneak it past her
Don't ever try to be funny
When she's counting dinner money
Don't ever make the big mistake
Of ever interrupting her at break

No one's worser – than the bursar
The never merry secretary
All the teachers seem to hate her
She's the school administrator
More beady eyes than a potato
A natural discriminator
Vicious cold interrogator
Staff claim form incinerator
She's the ruler – a dictator
She's the school administrator

Paul Cookson, David Harmer, Paula Harmer
(with a little help from Harriet Harmer too)

The Old Boiler

Conditions here are arctic
We're sitting in our coats
Miss has got the sniffles
We've all got sore throats

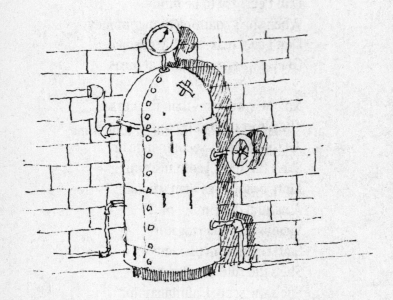

We're wearing gloves or mittens
We cannot hold our pens
I'm sure you get the picture
The boiler's failed again

Annually it happens
Every winter it's the same
The temperature's sub-zero
And the boiler is to blame

Thanks to the boiler
We all freeze
Thanks to the boiler
Our lessons cease

and we have to be sent home at lunchtime.
What a shame!

Thanks to the boiler
Long may it rule
Thanks to the boiler
Our boiler's *really* cool!

Bernard Young

It's the Gremlins

There are gremlins in the boiler house
Who put the fires out.
There are gremlins in the cupboards
Who move the furniture about.

They live in the piano
To put it out of tune;
And they make sure it rains on Sports Day –
The only wet day in June.

They play inside computers
And bring the system down.
They mix the paints when no one's looking
So that they all come out brown.

They're the ones who hide away your pen
And break the teacher's chalk;
They make sure *you're* the one caught for talking
When you're not supposed to talk!

And when the shed key's gone missing
Just before the start of games,
Well – by now – we know of course
Who really is to blame.

For when anything goes wrong,
In or around the school,
We know now that it's the gremlins,
For they're the ones who rule!

Alan Priestley

Miss Smith Rules – NOT!

'We'll have a Pet Day,' Miss Smith said.
'We'll study different creatures.'
She meant well, poor misguided soul –
One of those 'trusting' teachers.

Now with a normal class of course
It might have been all right,
But with the worst class in the school –
SHEER DYNAMITE!

It was Joe of course who set the trend,
With his spider quite spectacular,
But not one of the 'normal' kind –
A hairy big tarantula.

For that caused chaos straight away –
He took it out its box
And let it loose to crawl around –
Down one of Malik's socks.

Malik yelled and danced around
And trod on Hannah's goose.
It knocked a scorpion out Lee's hand –
Another killer loose!

Leroy's pit bull terrier
Had seen where it had gone –
It slipped its lead and made a charge
And swallowed it in one.

Marisa's ferret went berserk
And went for Joel's throat,
And the TV set was smashed to bits
By Faith's demented goat.

The Head stormed in and said, 'What's this?'
And tripped on Sharon's cat –
He did a sort of somersault
And fell flat on his back.

Chaos reigned for half an hour
With everybody screaming,
'Til all the pets were rounded up –
While Joe just sat there beaming.

The classroom was beyond repair,
Just like a bombed-out ruin,
And the Head yelled loud at poor Miss Smith,
'What the devil were you doing?'

He mopped his brow and looked around
At the damage that they'd done,
And yelled, 'You'd have been better off
With Attilla the Hun!'

And poor Miss Smith just sat and shook,
And shed another tear.
She said, 'I should have known of course –
It was perhaps a bad idea . . .'

Clive Webster

Don't Panic

Oh no, what will we dO?

Fear is spreading. What iF . . .

Scared head teacher quakes and shakeS

Teacher's hiding in the closeT

Everybody we arE

DOOMED

Roger Stevens

Breaktime Rules

Breaktime, breaktime
Everybody likes it
Teachers in the staffroom
Hugging steaming coffee mugs
Kids in the playground with
Footie games and kung fu
French skipping, card swapping
Who loves who.

Mrs Brown and Mrs Lee
Nattering together
Where they're going for their hols
What kind of weather
While down in the tool shed
Caretaker Fred
Reads his *Daily Mirror*
Puffs a cigarette.

Yes, breaktime's a great time.
Forget your science and maths
Assembly time, reading time
Horrible SATs.
The only time that matters
The best time of the day
Is breaktime.
BREAKTIME RULES. OK?

Patricia Leighton

Guess Who

When the Head is poorly
And has to stay in bed,
Things go on as normal –
There's still the Deputy Head.

And when one of the teachers
Has a day off school,
The other teachers split the class –
No problem as a rule.

So they're not that important,
They're never really missed –
It's someone else who's at the top
Of the 'Don't be absent' list.

For when this person's missing
There's chaos everywhere –
There's nobody to mop up blood
Or bathe your cuts with care.

There's no one there to ring the bells
Or take the money in,
Or sort out the lost property
Or find a safety pin.

Or phone up home if you're unwell,
Or show guests where to go,
Or hold your hand when you're upset
Or bandage up your toe.

So who's this super person
Who's missed more than the rest?
Who's more important than them all,
Who really is the best?

Who's nurse and doctor all in one,
And social worker too,
Teacher, friend and favourite aunt?
The Secretary – that's who!

Clive Webster

Who?

Who's always there come rain or shine,
From eight o'clock till ten past nine?
Who's back again at half past three
As we are going home for tea?

Who wears a coat that's long and white,
And cap with badge that's big and bright?
Who's always cheerful, always nice?
Whose banner bears a strange device?
Who teaches us the Highway Code,
And sees us safely 'cross the road?
Who is it makes the traffic stop?
O Lady of the Lollipop!

Colin West

Open Sesame

On the office wall
is a grey box and
in this grey box
are the school

KEYS

TO THE MAIN DOOR
BACK DOOR
SIDE DOOR
CRAFT STORE
GAMES STORE
KITCHEN STORE
COMPUTER ROOM
SCIENCE ROOM
BROOM
CUPBOARD
STAFF CUPBOARD
TROPHY CUPBOARD
COFFEE CUPBOARD
FIRST AID
GARDEN SPADES . . .

Yes, keys rule
this school
(as long as you have
the small, small key to
the box on the office
wall).

Patricia Leighton

The School Secretary's Day

The school secretary arrived at the crack of dawn
in order to guard the store cupboard in her office
from marauding teachers.
She checked her mantraps.
They were empty of any men
(or any women for that matter)
One had been sprung but there was only a toe in it.
She saw that the twenty or so locks, bolts
and padlocks on the store cupboard door were unsullied.
Satisfied, she opened it and shooed the mambas into
    their baskets.
She gazed upon the neat piles of boxes,
full of those accessories so greatly desired by teachers,
rubbers, scissors, notebooks . . .
Teachers arrived, spoiling the peace,
She prepared for battle.
It was *her* store cupboard.
'Rubbers!' she cried in amazement.
'Mr Pomfrey, your class had rubbers only last month.
I really can't release any more.'
Mr Pomfrey slunk away with a pronounced limp.
Next, a supply teacher (brought in to replace Miss Crumb)
came begging for drawing paper.
The school secretary gave him her special glare
and he went away.

Miss Crumb had stayed late, working, the previous evening.
An excuse to raid the store cupboard of course.
How else would the mambas have got her?
Nobody had any luck till the afternoon
when Mr Grimble, the maths co-ordinator
came away with a handful of rulers.
The wretched man had of course rescued the school secretary
from a raging bull only the day before.
'I think that this makes us even,' she said
as she handed them over.
The whole staffroom sent him to Coventry over it.
(The rescuing, not the rulers)
The Head had tried craftiness,
approaching the secretary's office with a bold tread.
'I've come to check the stores,' she lied.
'Surely you don't need more staples already,'
sneered the school secretary.
The Head stalked away, snapping an empty staple gun.
'Satisfactory day,' thought the school secretary,
'apart from the rulers.'
It was time to go.
She released the mambas,
locked, bolted and padlocked the storeroom door
and reset the man/woman traps.
As she left, she could hear the shuffling of feet,

the creaking of stays, and the puffing of the unfit.
A raiding party of teachers was gathering.
'Let them gather,' she thought,
'Let them gather.'
She ran a tight ship
but they respected her for it.
She jumped on to her cycle,
plucked a stray mamba from her corsets
and cycled into the sunset.

Marian Swinger

A selected list of titles available from Macmillan Children's Books

The prices shown below are correct at the time of going to press. However, Macmillan Publishers reserve the right to show new retail prices on covers which may differ from those previously advertised.

Who Rules the School?	0 330 35199 0	£3.50
The Secret Lives of Teachers	0 330 34265 7	£3.99
Top Secret Lives of Teachers	0 330 48345 5	£3.99
The Teacher's Revenge	0 330 39901 2	£3.99
The Very Best of Paul Cookson	0 330 48014 6	£3.99
You're Not Going Out Like That!	0 330 39846 6	£3.99
Don't Get Your Knickers in a Twist	0 330 39769 9	£3.99
Loony Letters and Daft Diaries	0 330 39847 7	£3.99
Ha Ha: Poems to Make You Laugh	0 330 39774 5	£4.99
What Shape is a Poem?	0 330 39707 9	£4.99
Ye New Spell Book	0 330 39708 7	£3.99
I Did Not Eat the Goldfish	0 330 39718 4	£3.99
Are We Nearly There Yet?	0 330 39767 2	£3.99
Taking My Human for a Walk	0 330 39871 7	£3.99
The Rhyme Riot	0 330 39900 4	£3.50
The Horrible Headmonster	0 330 48489 3	£3.50
My Stepdad's an Alien	0 330 41552 2	£3.99

All Macmillan titles can be ordered from our
website, www.panmacmillan.com,
or from your local bookshop and are also available by post from:
Bookpost, PO Box 29, Douglas, Isle of Man IM99 1BQ
Credit cards accepted. For details:
Telephone: 01624 836000
Fax: 01624 670923
E-mail: bookshop@enterprise.net
www.bookpost.co.uk
Free postage and packing in the United Kingdom